For pattern inquiries, please visit: www.go-crafty.com

Amigurumi Dolls

SPECIAL TECHNIQUE

adjustable ring method Holding the
yarn a few inches from the end, wrap
around your finger. Do not remove
wrap from finger, insert hook into the
wrap and draw up a loop of working
yarn. Chain one to secure the loop, and
remove ring from finger. Work stitches
of first round in the ring. Pull gently, but
firmly, on tail to tighten ring.

FINISHED MEASUREMENTS

Approx 6"/15cm tall

GAUGE

20 sc and 16 rounds = 4"/10cm using size
G/6 (4mm) crochet hook.
Take time to check gauge.

NOTE

When changing colors, draw new color
through 2 loops on hook to complete last sc.

RASPBERRY DOLL

Head

With A, make an adjustable ring.

Round 1 Work 6 sc in ring, do not join,
mark last st made with the safety pin;
tighten ring. You will now be working in a
spiral marking the last st made by moving
the safety pin up to indicate end of round.

Round 2 [Work 2 sc in next st] 6 times—
12 sts.

Round 3 [Sc in next st, work 2 sc in next
st] 6 times—18 sts.

Round 4 [Sc in next 2 sts, work 2 sc in
next st] 6 times—24 sts.

Round 5 [Sc in next 3 sts, work 2 sc in
next st] 6 times—30 sts.

Round 6 [Sc in next 4 sts, work 2 sc in
next st] 6 times—36 sts.

Rounds 7 and 8 Sc in each st around.

Round 9 [Sc2tog, sc in next 4 sts] 6
times—30 sts.

Round 10 [Sc2tog, sc in next 3 sts] 6
times—24 sts.

Round 11 [Sc2tog, sc in next 2 sts] 6
times—18 sts.

Round 12 [Sc2tog, sc in next st] 6 times,
end sl st in next st dropping safety pin—12
sts. Fasten off, leaving a 10"/25.5cm tail.

Body

With A, make an adjustable ring.

Rounds 1–4 Work as for head—24 sts.

Round 5 Working through back loops only,
sc in each st around.

Round 6 [Sc2tog, sc in next 4 sts] 4
times—20 sts.

Round 7 Sc in each st around.

Round 8 [Sc2tog, sc in next 3 sts] 4
times—16 sts.

Round 9 Repeat Round 7.

Round 10 [Sc2tog, sc in next st] 4 times,
end sl st in next st dropping safety pin—12
sts. Fasten off, leaving a 10"/25.5cm tail.

Feet (make 2)

With B, make an adjustable ring.

Rounds 1 and 2 Work as for head—12 sts.

Round 3 Sc in each st around.

Round 4 [Sc2tog] 6 times, end sl st in next
st dropping safety pin—6 sts.
Fasten off, leaving a 10"/25.5cm tail.

Arms (make 2)

Beginning at hand, with B, make an
adjustable ring.

Round 1 Work 5 sc in ring, do not join,
mark last st made with the safety pin;
tighten ring.

Round 2 [Work 2 sc in next st] 5 times—
10 sts.

Round 3 Sc in each st around.

Round 4 [Sc2tog] 5 times, changing to A in
last st—5 sts. Stuff hand with fiberfill.

Rounds 5 and 6 Repeat Round 3.

Round 7 Repeat Round 3, end sl st in next
st dropping safety pin. Fasten off leaving a
10"/25.5cm tail.

Ears (make 2)

With B, make an adjustable ring.
Rounds 1 and 2 Work as for arms—10 sts.
Rounds 3–6 Sc in each st around.
Round 7 Repeat round 3, end sl st in next st dropping safety pin. Fasten off, leaving a 10"/25.5cm tail.

Scarf

With C, ch 32.
Row 1 Turn to bottom loops of ch, hdc in 3rd loop from hook and in each loop across. Fasten off.

FINISHING

Weave in all loose ends, leaving tails for sewing. Stuff head, body and feet with fiberfill. Lining up the slip stitches of each piece, whipstitch head and body together, taking care to keep the stitches matched up. Whipstitch feet to body. Sew arms to top of body. Sew ears to top of head. Using thread doubled in sewing needle, sew on eyes. Using all six strands of red floss in embroidery needle, embroider a straight stitch mouth as shown. Tie scarf around neck.

GOLD DOLL

Head

Work as for Raspberry doll using D.

Body

Work as for Raspberry doll using E.

Feet (make 2)

Work as for Raspberry doll using D.

Arms (make 2)

Work as for Raspberry doll, working Rounds 1–4 using D, then changing to E at end of Round 4.

Ears (make 2)

Work as for Raspberry doll arms, working Rounds 1-4 using J, then changing to H at end of Round 4.

Scarf

Work as for Raspberry doll using F.

FINISHING

Work as for Raspberry doll.

PUMPKIN DOLL

Head
Work as for Raspberry doll using G.

Body
Work as for Raspberry doll using H.

Feet (make 2)
Work as for Raspberry doll using J.

Arms (make 2)
With J, make an adjustable ring.
Round 1 Work 5 sc in ring, do not join, mark last st made with the safety pin; tighten ring.
Round 2 [Work 2 sc in next st] 5 times—10 sts.
Round 3 Sc in each st around, changing to H in last st.
Rounds 4–6 Sc in each st around.
Round 7 Repeat round 4, end sl st in next st dropping safety pin. Fasten off leaving a 10"/25.5cm tail.

Ears (make 2)
Work as for Raspberry doll arms, working Rounds 1–4 using J, then changing to H at end of Round 4.

FINISHING

Weave in all the loose ends, leaving tails for sewing. Stuff head, body, arms and feet with fiberfill. Assemble pieces as for Raspberry doll. Using thread doubled in sewing needle, sew on eyes, then sew buttons to center front of body. Using all six strands of floss in embroidery needle, embroider a red straight stitch mouth and a black eyebrow over left eye as shown. ■

Flippy the Fish

STITCH GLOSSARY

sc3tog (single crochet 3 stitches
together) [Insert hook in next st, yarn
over and draw up a loop] 3 times, yarn
over and draw through all 4 loops on
hook.

SPECIAL TECHNIQUE

adjustable ring method Holding the
yarn a few inches from the end, wrap
around your finger. Do not remove
wrap from finger, insert hook into the
wrap and draw up a loop of working
yarn. Chain one to secure the loop, and
remove ring from finger. Work stitches
of first round in the ring. Pull gently, but
firmly, on tail to tighten ring.

FINISHED MEASUREMENTS

Approx 9"/23cm long (from mouth to tip of
tail) x 4½"/11.5cm high

GAUGE

Rounds 1–6 of body = 3¾"/9.5cm diameter.
Take time to check gauge.

NOTES

1 Body of fish is worked in continuous
spirals; do not join and do not turn at the
end of rounds. If desired, place a stitch
marker to indicate the beginning of the
round and move the stitch marker up as
each round is worked.

2 Gauge is not critical for this project. Work
tightly to ensure that fiberfill doesn't
show through stitches.

3 To change color, work last stitch of old
color to last yarn over, yarn over with
new color and draw through all loops on
hook. When working in rounds, carry colors
not in use loosely on wrong side of work. When working in
rows, fasten off old color.

BODY

Starting at mouth with D, form an
adjustable ring.

Round 1 (right side) Work 6 sc in ring; do
not join—6 sc.

Round 2 Work 2 sc in each sc around,
changing to A in last st—12 sc.

Round 3 With A, [sc in next sc, 2 sc in next
sc] 6 times—18 sc.

Round 4 [Sc in next 2 sc, 2 sc in next sc] 6
times—24 sc.

Round 5 [Sc in next 5 sc, 2 sc in next sc] 4
times—28 sc.

Round 6 [Sc in next 6 sc, 2 sc in next sc] 4
times—32 sc.

Round 7 [Sc in next 7 sc, 2 sc in next sc] 4
times—36 sc.

Round 8 [Sc in next 8 sc, 2 sc in next sc] 4
times, changing to D in last st—40 sc.

Round 9 With D, [sc in next 9 sc, 2 sc in next
sc] 4 times, changing to C in last st—44 sc.

Rounds 10–18 Sc in each sc around,
changing color in last st of appropriate
rounds as follows: work round 10 with C,
round 11 with D, rounds 12–14 with B,
round 15 with D, round 16 with C, round 17
with D, round 18 with B.

Round 19 With B, [sc in next 9 sc, sc2tog]
4 times—40 sc.
Begin stuffing fish, and continue stuffing as
work progresses.

Round 20 [Sc in next 8 sc, sc2tog] 4 times,
changing to D in last st—36 sc.

Round 21 With D, [sc in next 7 sc, sc2tog]
4 times, changing to C in last st—32 sc.

Round 22 With C, [sc in next 6 sc, sc2tog]
4 times, changing to D in last st—28 sc.

Round 23 With D, [sc in next 5 sc, sc2tog]
4 times, changing to B in last st—24 sc.

Round 24 With B, [sc in next 4 sc, sc2tog]
4 times—20 sc.

Round 25 [Sc in next 3 sc, sc2tog] 4
times—16 sc.

Round 26 [Sc in next 2 sc, sc2tog] 4 times,
changing to D in last st—12 sc. Do not
fasten off.

TAIL

Note Work now proceeds in rows.

Row 1 Flatten last round worked, folding
work between 1st/12th sc and 6th/7th
sc. With D, ch 1, working through both
thicknesses (to close body), sc in each sc
across, starting at 1st/12th sc and ending
at 6th/7th sc, changing to C in last st—6 sc.

Row 2 With C, ch 1, turn; sc in each sc
across, changing to D in last st.

Row 3 With D, ch 1, turn; 2 sc in first sc,
sc in each sc across to last sc, 2 sc in last
sc, changing to B in last st—8 sc.

Row 4 With B, ch 1, turn; sc in each sc
across.

Rows 5 and 6 Ch 1, turn; sc2tog, sc in
each sc across to last 2 sc, sc2tog,
changing to D in last st on row 6—4 sc at
end of row 6.

Row 7 With D, ch 1, turn; [sc2tog] twice,
changing to C in last st—2 sc.

Row 8 With C, ch 1, turn; sc2tog—1 sc.
Fasten off.

Flippy the Fish

Tail Edging
Join A with sl st in same st as first st on Row 1 of tail.

Row 1 Working in edges of rows along tail, ch 1, sk edge of Row 1, [(dc, ch 1, dc) in edge of next row, sk next row] 3 times, (dc, ch 1, dc, ch 1, dc) in sc on row 8 at tip of tail; working in edges of rows along opposite side of tail, sk next row, [(dc, ch 1, dc) in edge of next row, sk next row] 3 times, ch 1, sl st in same st as last st on Row 1 of tail.

Row 2 Ch 1, turn; sc in first ch-1 sp, work (ch 3, sc) in each st and ch-1 sp around tail; join with sl st in same st as first st on row 1 of tail. Fasten off.

FIN (MAKE 2)
Leaving a long tail, with B ch 4.

Row 1 Sc in 2nd ch from hook and in each remaining ch across, changing to D in last sc—3 sc.

Row 2 With D, ch 1, turn; sc in each sc across, changing to C in last sc.

Row 3 With C, ch 1, turn; sc in each sc across, changing to B in last sc.

Row 4 With B, ch 1, turn; sc in each sc across.

Row 5 Ch 1, turn; sc3tog—1 sc. Fasten off.

Fin Edging
Join A with sc in either edge of Row 1.

Row 1 Working in edges of rows along fin, ch 3, [sc in edge of next row, ch 3] 3 times, sk edge of Row 5, (sc, ch 3, sc) in sc on Row 5 at tip of fin; working in edges of rows along opposite side of fin, sk edge of Row 5, [ch 3, sc in edge of next row] 4 times. Fasten off.

EYE (MAKE 2)
With D, form an adjustable ring.

Round 1 (right side) Work 6 sc in ring, changing to C in last st; do not join.

Round 2 With C, sl st in back loop of each st around, changing to A in last st.

Round 3 With A, sl st in back loop of each st around. Fasten off, leaving a long tail for sewing. Gently tighten all ends, twist ends together and press into back of eye to stuff.

ASSEMBLY
With long tails, whipstitch fins to side of body, sewing first row of fins to Round 14 (3rd B-colored round). Using photographs as a guide, with long tails, sew eyes to top front of head about 1½"/4cmapart.

SHAPE MOUTH (OPTIONAL)
Thread a length of D, about 24"/61cm long, onto yarn needle. Identify two sts of Round 1 of fish that are directly across from each other horizontally. Insert needle into first of these sts and push needle all the way through body to base of tail. Draw end of length of D through. Remove needle from end of D and thread onto opposite end of length of D (still hanging out of mouth of fish). Insert needle into other st of Round 1 and push needle all the way through body to base of tail. Draw end of length of D through. Pull gently on both ends of D until mouth begins to pull into body of fish. Use fingers to shape mouth by pinching 'cheeks' on each side of mouth. When desired shape is achieved, firmly weave ends of D into base of tail.

FINISHING
Weave in all ends. ■

Bunny and Carrot

MATERIALS

Yarn 4

RED HEART® *Super Saver*®, 7oz/198g skeins, each approx 364yd/333m (acrylic)
1 skein each:
- #341 Light Grey (A)
- #724 Baby Pink (B)
- #254 Pumpkin (C)
- #368 Paddy Green (D)

Note Yarn quantities are sufficient to make several bunnies and carrots.

Hook
- Size 7 (4.5mm) crochet hook *or size to obtain gauge*

Notions
- 1 pair safety eyes—12mm diameter
- Stitch marker
- Polyester fiberfill
- Polyester pellets (for weight)
- 1 small red button
- Embroidery needle
- Yarn needle

FINISHED MEASUREMENTS
Bunny Approx 9"/23cm tall
Carrot Approx 8"/20.5cm tall

GAUGE
16 sc and 20 rounds = 4"/10cm.
Gauge is not critical for this project.

NOTES
1 This project is worked in continuous rounds, do not join and do not turn after completing a round.
2 Use a stitch marker to indicate the beginning of each round. Move the marker up as each round is completed. A pencil and notepad or a row counter can be used to keep track of the rounds worked.
3 Gauge is not critical for this project. However, work tightly to ensure that stuffing does not show through stitches.
4 For safety reasons, whenever making toys for children under 3 years of age, do not use safety eyes or buttons. Instead, embroider features. Make sure all pieces are sewn together securely and yarn ends are completely woven in and trimmed when finished.

BUNNY
Head
Beginning at top of head with A, ch 2.
Round 1 Work 6 sc in 2nd ch from hook—6 sc.
Round 2 2 sc in each sc around—12 sc.
Round 3 [2 sc in next sc, sc in next sc] 6 times—18 sc.
Round 4 [2 sc in next sc, sc in next 2 sc] 6 times—24 sc.
Round 5 [2 sc in next sc, sc in next 3 sc] 6 times—30 sc.
Round 6 [2 sc in next sc, sc in next 4 sc] 6 times—36 sc.
Round 7 [2 sc in next sc, sc in next 5 sc] 6 times—42 sc.
Round 8 [2 sc in next sc, sc in next 6 sc] 6 times—48 sc.
Rounds 9–22 Sc in each sc around.
Round 23 [Sc2tog, sc in next 6 sc] 6 times—42 sc.
Round 24 [Sc2tog, sc in next 3 sc] 8 times, sc2tog—33 sc.
Round 25 [Sc in next sc, sc2tog] 11 times—22 sc. Fasten off.
Attach safety eyes low on head and widely spaced. Stuff head firmly with polyester fiberfill.

Ears (make 2)
With A, ch 2.
Rounds 1–4 Work Rounds 1–4 of head—24 sc.
Rounds 5–14 Sc in each sc around.
Round 15 [Sc2tog, sc in next 2 sc] 6 times—18 sc.
Fasten off.
Pinch each ear at the base and sew together. Sew ears to top of the head.

Body
Beginning at bottom of body with A, ch 2.
Rounds 1–14 Work Rounds 1–14 of ear.
Fill body half way with polyester pellets then fill remainder of body with polyester fiberfill. Whipstitch body to bottom of head.

Arms and Legs (make 4)
With A, ch 2.
Round 1 Work 6 sc in 2nd ch from hook—6 sc.

Bunny and Carrot

Rounds 2–5 Sc in each sc around.
Fasten off.
Sew arms to sides of the body, where the body meets the head. Sew legs to the bottom of the body.

Dress
With B, ch 25; take care not to twist chain and join with sl st in first ch to form a ring.
Round 1 Sc in each ch around—25 sc.
Round 2 (armholes) Sc in first 4 sc, ch 4, sk next 4 sc, sc in next 9 sc, ch 4, sk next 4 sc, sc in next 4 sc—17 sc and 2 ch-4 sps.
Round 3 Sc in each sc and ch around—25 sc.
Rounds 4–10 Sc in each sc around.
Round 11 Sc in next sc, [ch 3, sk next sc, sc in next sc] 12 times—13 sc and 12 ch-3 sps.
Round 12 Sc in next sc, [3 sc in next ch-3 sp, sc in next sc] 12 times; sl st in first sc—49 sc. Fasten off.
Weave in ends. Slip dress onto body of bunny, slipping the arms through the armholes.

Flower
With B, ch 2.
Round 1 Work 5 sc in 2nd ch from hook—5 sc.
Round 2 (2 dc, sc) in each sc around—5 petals.
Fasten off.
Sew small red button into the center of the flower and sew the flower to the head.

CARROT
Beginning at tip of carrot with C, ch 2.
Round 1 Work 6 sc in 2nd ch from hook—6 sc.
Rounds 2 and 3 Sc in each sc around.
Round 4 2 sc in each sc around—12 sc.
Rounds 5–7 Sc in each sc around.
Round 8 [2 sc in next sc, sc in next sc] 6 times—18 sc.
Rounds 9–28 Sc in each sc around.
Round 29 [Sc2tog] 9 times. Fasten off.
Stuff carrot with polyester fiberfill. Sew top of carrot closed.

Leaves
With D, ch 2.
Round 1 Work 6 sc in 2nd ch from hook—6 sc.
Round 2 *Place marker in next sc, sc in marked sc, ch 10, dc in 2nd ch from hook, dc in next 3 ch, sc in last 5 ch, sc in marked sc (first leaf made); move marker to next sc of Round 1, sc in marked sc, ch 15, dc in 2nd ch from hook, dc in next 8 ch, sc in last 5 ch, sc in marked sc (second leaf made); repeat from * 2 more times, moving marker to next sc of Round 1 as each leaf is completed; sl st in first sc.
Fasten off.
Sew leaves to the top of the carrot.

FINISHING
Weave in all ends. ∎

Stitch Diagrams

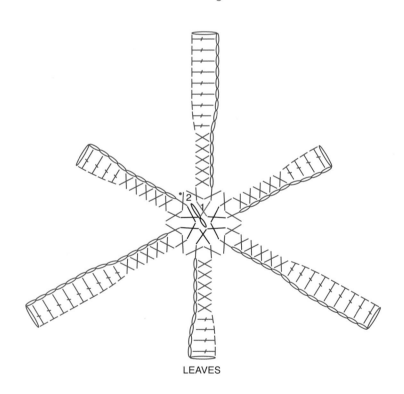

LEAVES

FLOWER

Wintertime Teddy

MATERIALS

Yarn 🧶**4**

RED HEART® *Fiesta*™, 6oz/170g skeins, each approx 316yd/289m (acrylic/nylon)
1 skein each:
- #6635 Coffee (A)
- #319 Cherry Red (C)

RED HEART® *Super Saver*®, 7 oz/198g skeins, each approx 364yd/333m (acrylic)
1 skein each:
- #313 Aran (B)

Hook
- Size G/6 (4mm) crochet hook *or size to obtain gauge*

Notions
- Doll safety eyes (with washers), 15mm diameter
- Polyester fiberfill stuffing
- Polyester stuffing pellets
- Stitch marker
- Yarn needle

FINISHED MEASUREMENTS
Approx 10"/25.5cm tall

GAUGE
18 sc and 24 rows with A = 4"/10cm.
Take time to check gauge.

NOTES
1 Exact gauge is not essential. Work tightly to ensure that stuffing does not show through stitches.
2 Bear is worked in continuous rounds; do not join and do not turn at beginning of rounds. Use a stitch marker to indicate beginning of each round; move marker up as work progresses.

HEAD
Beginning at top of head, with A, ch 2.
Round 1 Work 6 sc in 2nd ch from hook; do not join. Place marker to indicate beginning of round; move marker up as work progresses.
Round 2 2 sc in each sc around—12 sc.
Round 3 [2 sc in next st, sc in next st] 6 times—18 sc.
Round 4 [2 sc in next st, sc in next 2 sts] 6 times—24 sc.
Round 5 [2 sc in next st, sc in next 3 sts] 6 times—30 sc.
Round 6 [2 sc in next st, sc in next 4 sts] 6 times—36 sc.
Round 7 [2 sc in next st, sc in next 5 sts] 6 times—42 sc.
Round 8 [2 sc in next st, sc in next 6 sts] 6 times—48 sc.
Round 9 [2 sc in next st, sc in next 7 sts] 6 times—54 sc.
Round 10 [2 sc in next st, sc in next 8 sts] 6 times—60 sc.
Rounds 11–24 Sc in each st around.
Round 25 [Sc2tog, sc in next 8 sc] 6 times—54 sts.
Round 26 [Sc2tog, sc in next 4 sc] 9 times—45 sts.
Round 27 [Sc2tog, sc in next 3 sc] 9 times—36 sts.

Round 28 [Sc2tog, sc in next sc] 12 times—24 sts.
Round 29 [Sc2tog] 12 times—12 sts. Fasten off.

SNOUT
With B, ch 2.
Rounds 1–4 Work Rounds 1–4 of head—24 sc.
Rounds 5–8 Sc in each st around. Fasten off, leaving a long tail for sewing snout to head. Stuff snout with fiberfill and sew snout centered on front of head.

EAR (MAKE 2)
With A, ch 2.
Rounds 1–4 Work Rounds 1–4 of head—24 sc.
Rounds 5–9 Sc in each st around. Fasten off, leaving a long tail for sewing ears to head. Flatten ears and sew to the top of the head; gently bending the bottom of the ears into a "C" shape as you sew.

FACE
Eye Crescents (make 2)
With B, ch 3, work 9 tr in 3rd ch from hook; do not join.
Fasten off leaving a 6"/15cm tail.
Note Do not push stitches eye crescents into a complete circle. The side wedge of each eye crescent fits around the side of the snout.
Use doll eyes to attach eye crescents to head as follows: insert the peg of a doll eye into the ring at base of treble sts of each eye crescent; then push peg of doll eye through head to attach one eye on either side of snout, with center of eye aligned with center of snout. Secure doll eyes with washers. Use 6"/15cm tail to whip stitch edges of eye crescents to head. Stuff head firmly with fiberfill.

Nose and Smile
Cut an arm's length of A. Unravel the multicolored strand from the length of yarn and discard. With the photograph as

Wintertime Teddy

a guide, use remaining solid-colored portion of yarn and yarn needle to embroider a satin stitch nose and straight stitch smile.

BODY

With A, ch 36; taking care not to twist chain, join with a sl st in first ch to form a ring.
Round 1 Sc in each ch around; do not join. Place marker to indicate beginning of round; move marker up as work progresses.
Rounds 2–19 Sc in each st around.

First Leg

Round 20 Sc in first 18 sts, leave last 18 sts unworked (for second leg). Work now progresses in rounds worked over these first 18 sts only.
Rounds 21–30 Sc in each st around—18 sc.
Round 31 [2 sc in next st, sc in next st] 4 times, sc in last 10 sts—22 sc.
Rounds 32–35 Sc in each st around. Fasten off.

Second Leg

Round 20 Join A with sc in first unworked st following first leg; sc in each remaining unworked st around—18 sc.
Rounds 21–30 Sc in each st around—18 sc.
Round 31 [2 sc in next st, sc in next st] 4 times, sc in last 10 sts—22 sc.
Rounds 32–35 Sc in each st around. Fasten off.

SOLE OF FOOT (MAKE 2)

With A, ch 2.
Rounds 1–3 Work Rounds 1–3 of head—18 sc. Fasten off.
Note There are fewer sts in last round of sole than in last round of leg. This is to ensure that the bottoms of the feet don't bulge, which could cause a balance problem. Whipstitch soles of feet to ends of legs. Fill the body with weighted polyester pellets. Pour the pellets in and then press them into place to ensure the shape is completely filled and the bear is properly balanced. The head will be too heavy if the body is not sufficiently filled. Gather first round of body slightly and place head on top. Sew the head in place, taking care not to spill the pellets.

ARM (MAKE 2)

With A, ch 2.
Rounds 1–3 Work Rounds 1–3 of head—18 sc.
Rounds 4–20 Sc in each st around. Fasten off.
Fill arms with polyester pellets. This will add weight to the bear and help balance the size of the head. Flatten the top of the arm and sew shut. Sew top of arm to body where head meets the body.

SCARF

With C, ch 6.
Row 1 Dc in 3rd ch from hook (beginning ch counts as first dc), dc in each remaining ch—5 dc.
Row 2 Ch 2, turn, dc in each dc across. Repeat last row until scarf measures 20"/51cm. Fasten off.

FINISHING

If desired, make and sew 2"/5cm tassels to the ends of the scarf. Tie scarf around neck. Weave in all ends. ■

Tiny Teddies

Jack Deutsch

MATERIALS

Yarn (4)

RED HEART® *Baby TLC*,
6oz/170g skeins, each
approx 490yd/448m (acrylic)
1 skein each:
- #7625 Lime (A)
- #5945 Lilac (B)
- #5881 Powder Blue (C)
- #5935 Clear Blue (D)
- #5322 Powder Yellow (E)
- #5011 White (F)
- #5737 Powder Pink (G)

Hook
- Size D/3 (3.25mm) crochet hook *or size to obtain gauge*

Notions
- Polyester fiberfill
- Safety eyes, small buttons, or small amount of dark yarn
- Stitch marker
- Yarn needle

FINISHED MEASUREMENTS

Approx 5"/12.5cm tall from ears to legs x 2½"/6.5cm
wide from ear to ear

GAUGE

Rounds 1–4 on head = 1½"/4cm diameter.
Take time to check gauge.

BEAR

Ears (make 2)

With desired color, ch 3; join with sl st to form a ring.
Round 1 (right side) Work 7 sc in ring—7 sc.
Round 2 Work 2 sc in each of next 5 sc—10 sc. Fasten
off, leaving rem sts unworked and leaving a long tail.

Muzzle

With F, ch 3; join with sl st to form a ring.

Tiny Teddies

Round 1 (right side) Work 7 sc in ring—7 sc.
Round 2 Work 2 sc in each sc around—14 sc. Join with sl st in first sc. Fasten off, leaving a long tail.

Head and Body
Starting at top of head with desired color, ch 3; join with sl st to form a ring.
Round 1 (right side) Work 7 sc in ring—7 sc.
Round 2 Work 2 sc in each sc around—14 sc.
Round 3 [Sc in next sc, 2 sc in next sc] 7 times—21 sc.
Round 4 [Sc in next 2 sc, 2 sc in next sc] 7 times—28 sc.
Round 5 [Sc in next 3 sc, 2 sc in next sc] 7 times—35 sc.
Rounds 6–11 Sc in each sc around. Do not fasten off.

Head Assembly
Referring to photograph throughout assembly, sew flat edge of ears (unworked sts on Round 1) evenly spaced to top of head. Sew wrong side of muzzle to Rounds 7–11, evenly spaced between right side of ears. Add eyes to each side of muzzle with safety eyes, buttons or small amount of dark yarn. With G, stitch nose over muzzle.

Head and Body (continued)
Round 12 [Sc2tog, sc in next 3 sc] 7 times—28 sc.
Round 13 [Sc2tog, sc in next 2 sc] 7 times—21 sc.

Round 14 [Sc2tog, sc in next sc] 7 times—14 sc. Stuff head with fiberfill.
Round 15 [Sc2tog] 7 times—7 sc.
Rounds 16 and 17 Repeat Rounds 2 and 3.
Rounds 18–24 Sc in each sc around—21 sc.
Rounds 25 and 26 Repeat Rounds 14 and 15. At end of Round 26, fasten off, leaving a long tail.

Arms and Legs (make 4)
With same color as ears, ch 3; join with sl st to form a ring.
Round 1 (right side) Work 7 sc in ring—7 sc.
Rounds 2–4 Sc in each sc around. At end of round 4, fasten off, leaving a long tail.

FINISHING
Stuff body with fiberfill. Use tail to sew hole closed. Do not stuff arms and legs. Tuck beginning tails inside arms and legs, then sew end of arms and legs to body with ending tails. ■

> **TIP IDEAS**
> 1. Use a heavier weight yarn with corresponding hook, or lighter weight yarn with corresponding hook to get different size teddies!
>
> 2. In order to indicate the beg of a rnd, place a st marker on the first st of the rnd. When you finish a rnd, carry the marker up to indicate the beg.

Hoot Hoot Owl

FINISHED MEASUREMENTS
Approx 5½"/14cm high x 3¾"/9.5cm diameter

GAUGE
Rounds 1–4 on head = 2"/5cm diameter.
Take time to check gauge.

NOTES
1 Owl body and head are worked tightly in the round without joining. Place marker at beginning of round and move marker up to beginning of next round as work progresses.
2 It is helpful to keep track of the rounds you have worked with a pencil and paper or a row counter.
3 Doll eyes are not recommended for children under the age of three; in this case, embroider the eyes instead.

HEAD
Starting at top of head with A, ch 2.
Round 1 Work 6 sc in 2nd ch from hook—6 sc.
Round 2 Work 2 sc in each sc around—12 sc.
Round 3 *Work 2 sc in next sc, sc in next sc; repeat from * around—18 sc.
Round 4 *Work 2 sc in next sc, sc in next 2 sc; repeat from * around—24 sc.
Round 5 *Work 2 sc in next sc, sc in next 3 sc; repeat from * around—30 sc.
Round 6 *Work 2 sc in next sc, sc in next 4 sc; repeat from * around—36 sc.
Round 7 *Work 2 sc in next sc, sc in next 5 sc; repeat from * around—42 sc.
Round 8 *Work 2 sc in next sc, sc in next 6 sc; repeat from * around—48 sc.
Rounds 9–16 Sc in next sc and in each sc around.
Round 17 *Sc2tog, sc in next 6 sc; repeat from * around—42 sc.
Round 18 *Sc2tog, sc in next 5 sc; repeat from * around—36 sc.
Round 19 *Sc2tog, sc in next 4 sc; repeat from * around—30 sc.
Round 20 *Sc2tog, sc in next 3 sc; repeat from * around—24 sc.
Round 21 *Sc2tog, sc in next 2 sc; repeat from * around—18 sc.
Round 22 *Sc2tog, sc in next sc; repeat from * around—12 sc. Fasten off, leaving a long tail.

EYES (MAKE 2)
With C, ch 3.
Round 1 Work 12 dc in 3rd ch from hook—12 dc. Join with sl st in first dc. Fasten off, leaving 6"/15cm tail.

Head and Eye Assembly
Insert 18mm doll eyes into center of each crochet eye. Attach assembled eyes to head on Rounds 9–15, spacing eyes about 1"/2.5cm apart; secure with washers on inside of head. Stuff head very firmly. Do not skimp on stuffing! Whipstitch edges of crochet eyes onto head using 6"/15cm tails.

BODY
Starting at top of body with A, ch 18; being careful not to twist ch, join with sl st in first ch to form a ring.
Round 1 Ch 1; *2 sc in first ch, sc in next 2 chs; repeat from * around—24 sc.
Round 2 *Work 2 sc in next sc, sc in next 3 sc; repeat from * around—30 sc.
Round 3 *Work 2 sc in next sc, sc in next 4 sc; repeat from * around—36 sc.
Round 4 *Work 2 sc in next sc, sc in next 5 sc; repeat from * around—42 sc.
Rounds 5–13 Sc in next sc and in each sc around.
Round 14 *Sc2tog, sc in next 5 sc; repeat from * around—36 sc.
Round 15 *Sc2tog, sc in next 4 sc; repeat from * around—30 sc.
Round 16 *Sc2tog, sc in next 3 sc; repeat from * around—24 sc.
Round 17 *Sc2tog, sc in next 2 sc; repeat from * around—18 sc.
Round 18 *Sc2tog, sc in next sc; repeat from * around—12 sc.
Round 19 *Sc2tog; repeat from * around—6 sc. Fasten off, and close hole tightly with tail.

Hoot Hoot Owl

Head and Body Assembly

Add pellets to weight of body, if desired, then add fiberfill, or stuff body very firmly with only fiberfill. Whipstitch bottom of head to top of body.

WINGS (MAKE 2)

Starting at bottom of wing with C, ch 2.
Row 1 (right side) Sc in 2nd ch from hook—1 sc. Ch 1, turn.
Row 2 Work 2 sc in first sc—2 sc. Ch 1, turn.
Row 3 Work 2 sc in first sc, sc in next sc—3 sc. Ch 1, turn.
Row 4 Work 2 sc in first sc, sc in next sc and in each sc across—4 sc. Ch 1, turn.
Rows 5–12 Repeat Row 4 eight times more working one more sc in each row than in previous row. At end of Row 12—12 sc.
Round 1 Ch 1, sc evenly around all 3 edges of wing, increasing at corners as necessary. Join with sl st in first sc. Finish off, leaving a long tail.
Whipstitch top edge of wings to sides of body with right side of wings facing.

BEAK

Starting at bottom of beak with B, ch 2.
Rows 1–5 Work same as Rows 1–5 of wings. At end of Row 5, do not ch 1. Fasten off, leaving a long tail.
Whipstitch beak to head between eyes as shown in photograph.

FEET

With C and embroidery needle, stitch feet with straight stitches at base of body around Rounds 12–14.

FINISHING

Weave in all ends. ■

Birds of a Feather

MATERIALS

Yarn (4)

RED HEART® *Super Saver®*, 7oz/198g skeins, each approx 364yd/333m (acrylic)
1 skein each:
- #512 Turqua (A)
- #254 Pumpkin (B)
- #322 Pale Yellow (C)
- #312 Black (D)

Note Only small amounts of B, C, and D are needed

Hook
- Size H/8 (5mm) crochet hook *or size to obtain gauge*

Notions
- Polyester fiberfill
- Stitch marker (optional)
- Yarn needle

FINISHED MEASUREMENTS

Approx 5"/12.5cm tall (excluding comb) x 11"/28cm circumference (at chubbiest)

GAUGE

Rounds 1–13 of head and body (head) = 2½"/6.5cm diameter.
Gauge is not critical for this project.
Work tightly to ensure that stuffing doesn't show through stitches. If necessary, adjust hook size to obtain tight stitches.

NOTE

Head, body and beak are worked in continuous spirals; do not join and do not turn at the end of rounds. If desired, place a stitch marker to indicate the beginning of the round and move the stitch marker up as each round is worked.

BEAK

With B, ch 12; join with sl st in first ch to form a ring.
Round 1 Ch 1, sc in each ch around; do not join—12 sc.
Round 2 Sc in next sc, sc2tog, sc in next 5 sc, sc2tog, sc in last 2 sc—10 sc.
Round 3 [Sc in next 3 sc, sc2tog] twice—8 sc.
Round 4 [Sc2tog, sc in next 2 sc] twice—6 sc.
Round 5 [Sc in next sc, sc2tog] twice—4 sc. Fasten off, leaving a long tail. With tail, sew tip of beak closed and weave in end.

HEAD AND BODY

Beginning at top of head; with A, ch 4; join with sl st in first ch to form a ring.
Round 1 Work 7 sc in ring; do not join.
Round 2 2 sc in each sc around—14 sc.
Round 3 [Sc in next sc, 2 sc in next sc] 7 times—21 sc.
Round 4 [Sc in next 2 sc, 2 sc in next sc] 7 times—28 sc.
Round 5 [Sc in next 3 sc, 2 sc in next sc] 7 times—35 sc.
Rounds 6–10 Sc in each sc around.
Round 11 [Sc2tog, sc in next 3 sc] 7 times—28 sc.
Firmly stuff beak and sew to center of face (approx between Rounds 6 and 9). With D, embroider eye on either side of upper edge of beak (refer to photograph). Firmly stuff head; continue to stuff head and body as work progresses.
Round 12 [Sc2tog, sc in next 2 sc] 7 times—21 sc.
Round 13 [Sc2tog, sc in next sc] 7 times—14 sc.
Rounds 14–16 Repeat Rounds 3–5—35 sc.

Birds of a Feather

Rounds 17–24 Sc in each sc around.
Rounds 25–27 Repeat Rounds 11–13—14 sc.
Round 28 [Sc2tog] 7 times—7 sc. Fasten off, leaving a long tail. Finish stuffing body. Weave tail through stitches of last round, pull tight and secure. Weave in tail.

WING (MAKE 2)

With A, ch 8.
Row 1 Sc in 2nd ch from hook and in each remaining ch across—7 sc.
Rows 2 and 3 Ch 1, turn, sc in each sc across.
Row 4 Ch 2, turn, sc in 2nd ch from hook, skip first sc, sc in next sc (first feather); ch 3, sc in 2nd ch from hook and in next ch, sc in next sc (second feather); ch 4, sc in 2nd ch from hook and in next 2 ch, sc in next sc (third feather); ch 5, sc in 2nd ch from hook and in next 3 ch, sc in next sc (fourth feather); ch 6, sc in 2nd ch from hook and in next 4 ch, skip next sc, sl st in next sc (fifth feather). Fasten off, leaving a long tail for sewing wings to sides of body.

FOOT (MAKE 2)

With C, ch 6.
Row 1 Sc in 2nd ch from hook and in each remaining ch across—5 sc.
Row 2 Ch 1, turn, sc in each st across.
Row 3 Ch 1, turn, (sc, hdc, dc, hdc, sc) in each of next 3 sts, sl st in last 2 sts. Fasten off leaving a long tail for sewing feet to lower front of body.

TAIL

With A, ch 7.
Rows 1–3 Work as for Rows 1–3 of wing—6 sc.
Row 4 Ch 4, turn, sc in 2nd ch from hook and in next 2 ch, skip first sc, sc in next sc (first feather); ch 6, sc in 2nd ch from hook and in next 4 ch, sc in next sc (second feather); ch 8, sc in 2nd ch from hook and in next 6 ch, sc in next sc (third feather); ch 6, sc in 2nd ch from hook and in next 4 ch, sc in next sc (fourth feather); ch 4, sc in 2nd ch from hook and in next 2 ch, sl st in next sc (fifth feather). Fasten off, leaving a long tail for sewing tail to lower back of body.

COMB (OPTIONAL)

With A, ch 6.
Rows 1–3 Work as for Rows 1–3 of wing—5 sc.
Row 4 Ch 4, turn, sc in 2nd ch from hook and in next 2 ch, skip first sc, sc in next sc (first feather); ch 6, sc in 2nd ch from hook and in next 4 ch, sc in next sc (second feather); ch 8, sc in 2nd ch from hook and in next 6 ch, sc in next sc (third feather); ch 9, sc in 2nd ch from hook and in next 7 ch, sl st in last sc (fourth feather). Fasten off, leaving a long tail for sewing comb to top of head.

FINISHING

With long tails, whipstitch wings to side of body, tail to lower back of body, feet to lower front of body and comb (optional) to top of head. ■

Stitch Diagrams

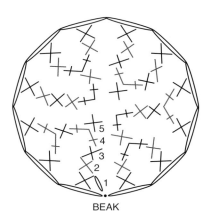
BEAK

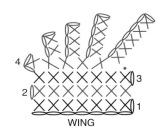
WING

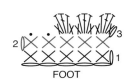
FOOT

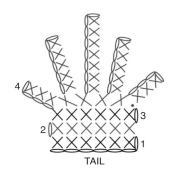
TAIL

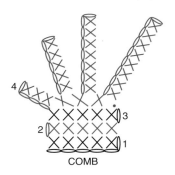
COMB

Mischievous Monkeys

FINISHED MEASUREMENTS

Monkey Approx 8"/20.5cm tall x 5¼"/13.3cm around belly

Hat Approx 3"/7.5cm tall x 7"/18cm around opening

GAUGE

Gauge is not critical for this project.

NOTES

1 Monkey can be made in choice of Windsor Blue, Dark Orchid or Coffee. Throughout pattern, A refers to your choice of body color.
2 Body and head worked as one piece, from top to bottom. Arms, legs, ears, tail and face stitched separately, then sewn to body. All pieces worked in the round.
3 Use stitch marker to keep track of rounds. Move it up every round, placing it in last st of round just worked.

BODY AND HEAD

Beginning at top of head, with A, ch 2.
Round 1 Work 6 sc in 2nd ch from hook, mark end of round—6 sts.
Round 2 Work 2 sc in each sc around—12 sts.
Round 3 *Sc in next st, work 2 sc in next st; repeat from * around—18 sts.
Round 4 *Sc in next 2 sts, work 2 sc in next st; repeat from * around—24 sts.
Round 5 Sc in next 5 sts, [work 2 sc in next st] twice, sc in next 10 sts, [work 2 sc in next st] twice, sc in each st around—28 sts.
Round 6 Sc in each st around.
Round 7 Sc in next 6 sts, [work 2 sc in next st] twice, sc in next 12 sts, [work 2 sc in next st] twice, sc in each st around—32 sts.
Rounds 8–10 Sc in each st around.
Round 11 Sc in next 6 sts, [sc2tog] twice, sc in next 13 sts, [sc2tog] twice, sc in each st around—28 sts.
Round 12 Sc in each st around.
Round 13 Sc in next 5 sts, [sc2tog] twice, sc in next 11 sts, [sc2tog] twice, sc in each st around—24 sts.
Round 14 Sc in next 6 sts, sc2tog, sc in next 9 sts, sc2tog, sc in each st around—22 sts.
Rounds 15–24 Sc in each st around.
Round 25 Sc in next 4 sts, sc2tog, sc in next 11 sts, sc2tog, sc in each st around—20 sts.
Round 26 *Sc in next 3 sts, sc2tog; repeat from * around—16 sts.
Fill piece with fiberfill.
Round 27 *Sc in next 2 sts, sc2tog; repeat from * around—12 sts.
Round 28 Sc2tog around—6 sts. Fasten off. Weave end through top of sts and pull to tighten. Weave in end.

EAR (MAKE 2)

With A, ch 2.
Round 1 Work 6 sc in 2nd ch from hook, mark end of round—6 sts.
Round 2 Work 2 sc in each st around—12 sts.
Rounds 3–5 Sc in each st around.
Fasten off.

TAIL

With A, ch 28.
Row 1 Sc in 2nd ch from hook and in each ch to end—27 sts. Fasten off.

ARM OR LEG (MAKE 4)

With A, ch 2.
Round 1 Work 8 sc in 2nd ch from hook, mark end of round—8 sts.
Rounds 2–15 Sc in each sc around. Fasten off.

FACE

With B, ch 2.
Round 1 Work 6 sc in 2nd ch from hook—6 sts.
Round 2 Work 2 sc in each sc around—12 sts.
Round 3 *Sc in next st, work 2 sc in next st; repeat from * around—18 sts.
Round 4 *Sc in next 2 sts, work 2 sc in next st; repeat from * around—24 sts.
Round 5 *Sc in next 3 sts, work 2 sc in next st; repeat from * around—30 sts.
Turn.

Mischievous Monkeys

Note Do not ch 1 at beginning of Round 6, to create a notch in the last round.
Round 6 Sc in each st around. Do not join at end of round. Fasten off.

FINISHING
Weave in ends. Embroider mouth, eyes and nose on face, as shown in picture. Fill body parts with polyester fiberfill stuffing. With matching sewing thread, sew face to center front of head, with notch at top. With matching yarn, sew ears to sides of head, and sew arms, legs and tail to body.

SANTA HAT
With C, ch 2.
Round 1 Work 6 sc in 2nd ch from hook, mark end of round—6 sts.
Rounds 2–3 Sc in each sc around.
Round 4 Work 2 sc in each st around—12 sts.

Round 5 Sc in each st around.
Round 6 *Sc in next st, work 2 sc in next st; repeat from * around—18 sts.
Round 7 *Sc in next 2 sts, work 2 sc in next st; repeat from * around—24 sts.
Round 8 Sc in each st around.
Round 9 *Sc in next 3 sts, work 2 sc in next st; repeat from * around—30 sts.
Round 10 Sc in each st around.
Change to D.
Rounds 11 and 12 Sc in each st around. Weave in ends. Fasten off.

POM-POM
With D, ch 2.
Round 1 Work 8 sc in 2nd ch from hook, mark end of round—8 sts.
Rounds 2–4 Sc in each st around. Remove marker. Cut ends of yarn to about 4"/10.2cm long and tuck inside pom-pom to stuff. Sew pom-pom to top of Santa hat. ■

Under the Sea

MATERIALS

Yarn 4

RED HEART® *Baby TLC*, 5oz/141g skeins, each approx 358yd/328m 1 skein each:
- #5945 Lilac (A)
- #7625 Lime (B)
- Small amount #5011 White (C)

Hooks
- Size E/4 (3.5mm) crochet hook *or size to obtain gauge*
- Size C/2 (2.75mm) crochet hook

Notions
- Stitch markers
- Small amount of black yarn (to embroider pupil)
- Polyester fiberfill
- Yarn needle

STITCH GLOSSARY

inv-dec (invisible decrease) Insert hook in front loop only of next 2 stitches, yarn over and draw through all loops on hook.

FINISHED MEASUREMENTS

Approx 15"/38cm diameter (at widest) x 14"/35.5cm long (from top of head to end of tentacles)

GAUGE

Rounds 1–9 = 4"/10cm diameter using size E/4 (3.5mm) crochet hook.
Take time to check gauge.

NOTES

1 The octopus body and eyes are worked in continuous rounds. Do not join or turn at the end of rounds. Place a stitch marker to indicate beginning of round; move marker up as work progresses.
2 The octopus spots are worked in joined rounds.
3 Gauge is not essential for this project. Work tightly to ensure that stuffing will not show through stitches.
4 For extra, tiny spots (as in photo), embroider with a yarn needle and yarn B.

BODY

With larger hook and A, ch 3; join with sl st in first ch to form a ring.

Round 1 Work 7 sc in ring—7 sc. Place a stitch marker to indicate beginning of round; move marker up as work progresses.
Round 2 2 sc in each st around—14 sts.
Round 3 [Sc in next st, 2 sc in next st] 7 times—21 sts.
Round 4 [Sc in next 2 sts, 2 sc in next st, place stitch marker in 2nd sc of 2 sc just made] 7 times—28 sts.
Round 5 [Sc in each st to next marked st, 2 sc in marked st, move marker to 2nd sc of 2 sc just made] 7 times—35 sts.
Rounds 6–11 Repeat Round 5—77 sts. Remove all markers except beginning of round marker.
Rounds 12–17 Sc in each st around.
Round 18 Sc in next 10 sts, inv-dec, sc in each rem st around—76 sts.
Round 19 Sc in next 15 sts, inv-dec, place marker in inv-dec just made, sc in each rem st around—75 sts.
Round 20 Sc in each st to marked st,

Under the Sea

remove marker, sc in marked inv-dec, sc in next 4 sts, inv-dec, place marker in inv-dec just made, sc in each rem st around—74 sts.
Rounds 21–28 Repeat Round 20—66 sts.
Round 29 Sc in next 5 sts, inv-dec, place marker in inv-dec just made, sc in each rem st around—65 sts.
Rounds 30–34 Sc in each st to marked st, remove marker, sc in marked inv-dec, sc in next 4 sts, inv-dec, place marker in inv-dec just made, sc in each rem st around—60 sts.
Rounds 35–42 Sc in each st around.
Fasten off and weave in end.

EYE (MAKE 2)
With smaller hook and C, ch 3; join with sl st in first ch to form a ring.
Round 1 Work 7 sc in ring—7 sc. Place a stitch marker to indicate beginning of round; move marker up as work progresses
Round 2 2 sc in each st around—14 sts. Fasten off, leaving a long tail for sewing eye to body. Flatten body and pin one eye about ½"/1.5cm from each side edge and about 1"/2.5cm above lower edge. Sew eyes in place. With small amount of black yarn, embroider pupils on eyes. With small amount of C, embroider white flecks (reflection) on pupils (refer to photograph). Hide ends inside body.

LARGE SPOT (MAKE 2)
With smaller hook and B, ch 3; join with sl st in first ch to form a ring.
Round 1 Ch 3 (counts as dc), work 15 more dc in ring; join with sl st in top of beginning ch—16 dc.
Round 2 Ch 1, 2 sc in same st as join, sc in next st, [2 sc in next st, sc in next st] 7 times; join with sl st in first sc—24 sts. Fasten off, leaving a long tail for sewing spots to body. Sew spots on top and front of body (refer to photograph for placement).

SMALL SPOT (MAKE 1)
With smaller hook and B, ch 3; join with sl st in first ch to form a ring.
Round 1 Ch 2 (counts as hdc), work 15 more hdc in ring; join with sl st in top of beginning ch—16 hdc.

Fasten off, leaving a long tail for sewing spot to body. Sew spot on front of body (refer to photograph for placement).

LEGS
With right side facing and larger hook and A, join yarn with sl st in last round of body at center back.
Round 1 Ch 1, sc in same st as join, sc in next 5 sts; [ch 39, dc in 3rd ch from hook and in each rem ch across, sk next st on last round of body, sc in next 6 sts on last round of body] 7 times; ch 39, dc in 3rd ch from hook and in each rem ch across, sk next st on last round of body, sc in each rem st on last round of body; join with sl st in first sc—8 legs started.
Round 2 Ch 1, sc in next 6 body sts, [hdc in next 36 leg sts, sc in last leg st, sc in ch-2 beginning ch; working along opposite side of leg stitches, in next 12 ch, hdc in next 12 ch, dc in each rem ch across, sk next body st, sc in next 5 body sts] 7 times; hdc in next 36 leg sts, sc in last leg st, sc in ch-2 beginning ch; working along opposite side of leg stitches, sc in next 12 ch, hdc in next 12 ch, dc in each rem ch across, sk next body st, sc in each rem body st; join with sl st in first sc. Fasten off.
Round 3 Join B with sl st in same st as join of Round 2, ch 1, sc in each st around all edges; join with sl st in first sc. Fasten off and weave in end.

BOTTOM (MAKE 1)
With larger hook and A, ch 3; join with sl st in first ch to form a ring.
Rounds 1–9 Work Rounds 1–9 of body—63 sts.
Fasten off, leaving a long tail for sewing.

FINISHING
Stuff body firmly. With yarn needle and long tail sew bottom to lower edge of body, inside leg rounds.
Weave in all ends. ■

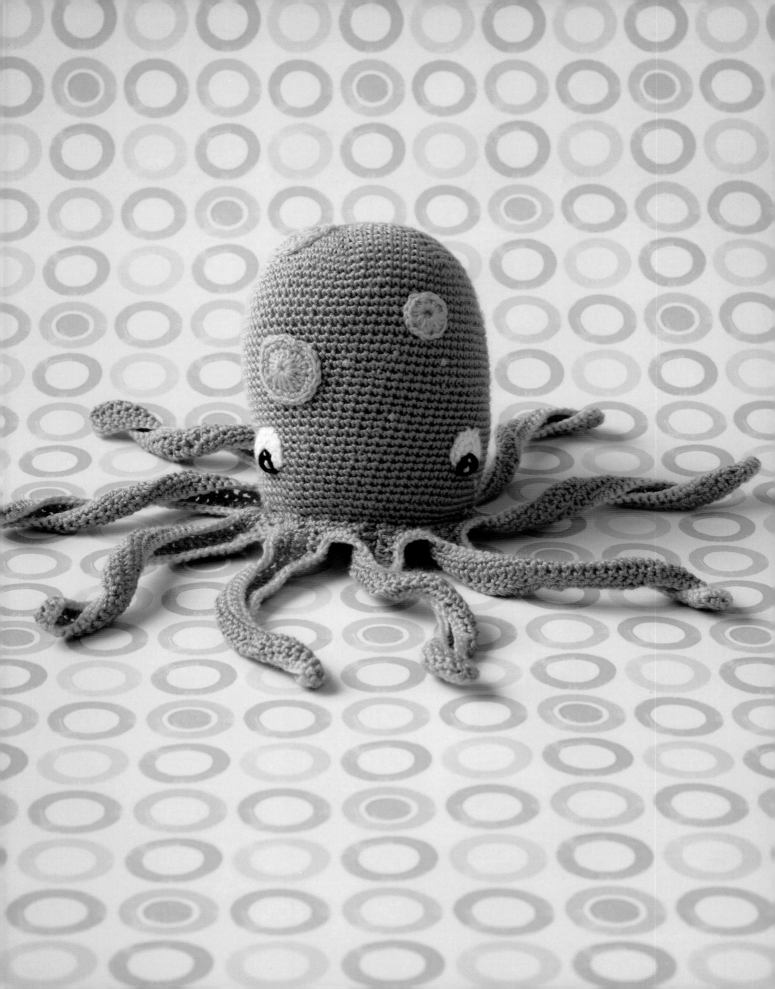

Clock

MATERIALS

Yarn 🔵**4**

RED HEART® *Super Saver*®,
7oz/198g skeins, each approx
364yd/333m (acrylic)
1 skein each:
- #316 Soft White (A)
- #319 Cherry Red (B)
- #341 Light Grey (C)

Note Yarn quantities are sufficient
to make several alarm clocks.

Hook
- Size G/6 (4mm) crochet hook *or
  any size to obtain correct gauge*

Notions
- 1 pair safety eyes—¼"/6mm
  diameter
- Stitch marker
- Polyester fiberfill
- Small quantities of red and black
  embroidery floss
- Small piece of black felt
- Small quantity of black sewing
  thread
- Sewing needle
- Yarn needle

FINISHED MEASUREMENTS

Approx 7"/18cm tall

GAUGE

Rounds 1–6 of face = 4"/10cm diameter.
Gauge is not critical for this project.
However, work tightly to ensure that
stuffing does not show through stitches.
If necessary, adjust hook size to obtain
correct tension.

NOTES

1 This project is worked in continuous
  rounds. Do not join and do not turn after
  completing a round.
2 Use a stitch marker to indicate the beginning of each round. Move the marker up

as each round is completed. A pencil and
note pad or a row counter can be used
to keep track of the rounds worked.

3 For safety reasons, whenever making
  toys for children under 3 years of age, do
  not use safety eyes or buttons. Instead,
  embroider features. Make sure all
  pieces are sewn together securely and
  yarn ends are completely woven in and
  trimmed when finished.

4 To change color, work last stitch of old
  color to last yarn over. Yarn over with new
  color and draw through all loops on hook
  to complete stitch. Fasten off old color.

FACE

With A, ch 2.

Round 1 Work 6 sc in 2nd ch from
hook—6 sc.

Round 2 2 sc in each sc around—12 sc.

Round 3 [Sc in next sc, 2 sc in next sc] 6
times—18 sc.

Round 4 [Sc in next 2 sc, 2 sc in next sc] 6
times—24 sc.

Round 5 [Sc in next 3 sc, 2 sc in next sc] 6
times—30 sc.

Round 6 [Sc in next 4 sc, 2 sc in next sc] 6
times—36 sc.

Round 7 [Sc in next 5 sc, 2 sc in next sc] 6
times—42 sc.

Round 8 [Sc in next 6 sc, 2 sc in next sc] 6
times; change to B in last st—48 sc.

Embellish Face

Following package instructions, and using
photograph as guide for placement, attach
safety eyes. With black embroidery floss,
embroider mouth. With red embroidery
floss, embroider "second" hand. Cut a
piece of felt 2 x ¼"/5 x 0.5cm for "hour"
hand, and another piece of felt 1½ x ¼"/4 x
0.5cm for "minute" hand. With black
sewing thread, sew hands to face.

Continue Face

Round 9 With B and working through back
loops only, [sc in next 7 sc, 2 sc in next sc]
6 times—54 sc.

Rounds 10–16 Sc in each sc around.
Sl st in next st. Fasten off, leaving a
28"/71cm tail for sewing.

BACK

With B, ch 2.

Rounds 1–8 With B, work Rounds 1–8 of
face—48 sc.

Round 9 [Sc in next 7 sc, 2 sc in next sc] 6
times—54 sc.

Sl st in next st. Fasten off.

BELL (MAKE 2)

With C, ch 2.

Rounds 1–5 With C, work Rounds 1–5 of
face—30 sc.

Rounds 6 and 7 Sc in each sc around.

Round 8 [Sc in next 3 sc, sc2tog] 6
times—24 sts.

Sl st in next st. Fasten off, leaving a
14"/35.5cm tail for sewing.

BELL CONNECTOR

Leaving a 6"/15cm beginning tail for sewing, and holding 2 strands of C together,
ch 22. Fasten off, leaving a 6"/12cm tail for
sewing.

FOOT (MAKE 4)

With B, ch 2.

Round 1 Work 7 sc in 2nd ch from
hook—7 sc.

Round 2 Working in back loops only, sc in
each sc around.

Rounds 3 and 4 Sc in each sc around.
Sl st in next st. Fasten off, leaving a
9"/23cm tail for sewing.

FINISHING

Using long tail from face, sew back and
face together about three quarters of the
way around. Stuff firmly with polyester
fiberfill and complete sewing back and face
together. Using tails, sew one end of bell
connector to center top of each bell. Stuff
bells lightly. Using long tails, sew bells to
top of clock. Stuff feet lightly. Using tails,
sew feet to bottom of clock.
Weave in all ends. ■

Fairy & Gnome Dolls

FINISHED MEASUREMENTS

Fairy Approx 8"/20.5cm tall
Gnome Approx 10"/25.5cm tall without hat (hat adds about 1"/2.5cm)

GAUGE

Gauge is not critical for this project.

NOTES

1 Work tightly so stuffing will not show through stitches.
2 Rounds are worked in continuous spirals. Do not join at end of rounds and do not turn at beginning of rounds.
3 To change color, work last stitch of old color to last yarn over. Yarn over with new color and draw through all loops on hook to complete stitch. Fasten off old color and proceed with new color.

FAIRY

Head

Beginning at top of head, with D, ch 2.
Round 1 (right side) 5 sc in 2nd ch from hook; do not join, work in continuous rounds—5 sc. Place a marker for beginning of round and move marker up as work progresses.
Round 2 Work 2 sc in each sc around—10 sc.
Round 3 [Sc in next sc, 2 sc in next sc] 5 times—15 sc.
Round 4 [Sc in next 2 sc, 2 sc in next sc] 5 times—20 sc.
Round 5 [Sc in next 3 sc, 2 sc in next sc] 5 times—25 sc.
Round 6 [Sc in next 4 sc, 2 sc in next sc] 5 times—30 sc.
Round 7 [Sc in next 5 sc, 2 sc in next sc] 5 times—35 sc.
Rounds 8–16 Sc in each sc around.
Round 17 [Sc in next 5 sc, sc2tog] 5 times—30 sc.
Round 18 [Sc in next 4 sc, sc2tog] 5 times—25 sc.
Round 19 Sc in each sc around.
Position and attach safety eyes. With red embroidery floss and using photograph as a guide, embroider smile. With brown embroidery floss, embroider nose.

Round 20 [Sc in next 3 sc, sc2tog] 5 times—20 sc.
Round 21 [Sc in next 2 sc, sc2tog] 5 times—15 sc.
Stuff head.
Round 22 [Sc in next sc, sc2tog] 5 times—10 sc.
Round 23 [Sc2tog] 5 times—5 sc.
Fasten off.

Body

Beginning at bottom of body, with C, ch 2.
Round 1 (right side) 6 sc in 2nd ch from hook; do not join, work in continuous rounds—6 sc. Place a marker for beginning of round and move marker up as work progresses.
Round 2 Work 2 sc in each sc around—12 sc.
Round 3 [Sc in next sc, 2 sc in next sc] 6 times—18 sc.
Rounds 4–6 Sc in each sc around.
Round 7 Working in back loops only, sc in each sc around.
Rounds 8–12 Sc in each sc around.
Sl st in next sc.
Fasten off, leaving a long tail for sewing. Stuff body. With tail, sew body to bottom of head.

Leg (make 2)

Beginning at foot, with C, ch 2.
Round 1 (right side) 6 sc in 2nd ch from hook; do not join, work in continuous rounds—6 sc. Place a marker for beginning of round and move marker up as work progresses.
Round 2 Sc in each sc around; change to D in last st—12 sc.
Stuff leg as Rounds 3–10 are worked.
Rounds 3–10 Sc in each sc around.
Fasten off, leaving a long tail for sewing. Sew leg to bottom of body.

Arm (make 2)

Beginning at hand, with D, ch 2.
Round 1 (right side) 6 sc in 2nd ch from hook; do not join, work in continuous rounds—6 sc. Place a marker for beginning of round and move marker up as work progresses.
Rounds 2–8 Sc in each sc around.

Fasten off, leaving a long tail for sewing.
Flatten open end and sew closed.
Sew arm to side of body, near where body meets head.

Skirt

Top edge
Hold fairy upside down (legs in the air), join A with sc in any of the unworked front loops at back of Round 6 of body, sc in remaining 17 sc—18 sc.
Fasten off and weave in end.

Petal (make 6)
With A, ch 2.
Round 1 (right side) 6 sc in 2nd ch from hook; do not join, work in continuous rounds—6 sc. Place a marker for beginning of round and move marker up as work progresses.
Round 2 Sc in each sc around.
Round 3 Work 2 sc in each sc around—12 sc.
Rounds 4–6 Sc in each sc around.
Round 7 [Sc2tog] 6 times—6 sc.
Sl st in next sc.
Fasten off, leaving a long tail for sewing.
Flatten open end and sew closed.
Sew petals evenly spaced to top edge of skirt.

Large Upper Wing (make 2)
With F, ch 2.
Round 1 (right side) 6 sc in 2nd ch from hook; do not join, work in continuous rounds—6 sc. Place a marker for beginning of round and move marker up as work progresses.
Round 2 Sc in each sc around.
Round 3 [Sc in next sc, 2 sc in next sc] 3 times—9 sc.
Round 4 Sc in each sc around.
Round 5 [Sc in next 2 sc, 2 sc in next sc] 3 times—12 sc.
Rounds 6–14 Sc in each sc around.
Round 15 [Sc2tog] 6 times—6 sc.
Sl st in next sc.
Fasten off, leaving a long tail for sewing.

Small Lower Wing (make 2)
With F, ch 2.
Rounds 1–6 Work Rounds 1–6 of large upper wings.
Round 7 [Sc2tog] 6 times—6 sc.
Round 8 Sc in each sc around.
Sl st in next sc.
Fasten off, leaving a long tail for sewing.

FINISHING
Flatten upper and lower wings and arrange on back of Fairy.
Sew wings in place.

Hair
Cut strands of B twice as long as desired length of hair. Fold one strand in half, insert crochet hook around post of a stitch on top of head and then into fold of strand. Draw fold through, forming a loop. Insert ends of strand through loop and pull gently to tighten. Repeat this process to create several rows of hair along top of head. Allow the strands to fall to the sides, and attach the number of strands needed for desired thickness of hair. Collect hair into two pigtails and secure with Little Flowers.

Little Flowers (make 2)
With E, [ch 4, hdc in 3rd ch from hook, sl st in next ch] 4 times.
Fasten off, leaving a long tail.
Use tail to sew petals into a ring to form flower. Tie flower around half of hair to hold pigtail. Weave in any remaining ends.

GNOME
Head
Beginning at top of head, with G, ch 2.
Round 1 (right side) 6 sc in 2nd ch from hook; do not join, work in continuous rounds—6 sc. Place a marker for beginning of round and move marker up as work progresses.

Round 2 Work 2 sc in each sc around—12 sc.
Round 3 [Sc in next sc, 2 sc in next sc] 6 times—18 sc.
Round 4 [Sc in next 2 sc, 2 sc in next sc] 6 times—24 sc.
Round 5 [Sc in next 3 sc, 2 sc in next sc] 6 times—30 sc.
Round 6 [Sc in next 4 sc, 2 sc in next sc] 6 times—36 sc.
Rounds 7–18 Sc in each sc around.
Round 19 [Sc in next 4 sc, sc2tog] 6 times—30 sc.
Round 20 [Sc in next 3 sc, sc2tog] 6 times—24 sc.
Position and attach safety eyes. With red embroidery floss and using photograph as a guide, embroider smile. With brown embroidery floss, embroider nose.
Round 21 [Sc in next 2 sc, sc2tog] 6 times—18 sc.
Stuff head.
Round 22 [Sc in next sc, sc2tog] 6 times—12 sc.
Round 23 [Sc2tog] 6 times—6 sc.
Fasten off.

Body
Beginning at bottom of body, with J, ch 2.
Rounds 1–4 Work Rounds 1–4 of head—24 sc.
Rounds 5–7 Sc in each sc around; change to I in last st of Round 7.
Round 8 Sc in each sc around.
Round 9 Working in back loops only, sc in each sc around.
Rounds 10 and 11 Sc in each sc around.
Round 12 [Sc in next 2 sc, sc2tog] 6 times—18 sc.
Rounds 13–16 Sc in each sc around.
Sl st in next sc.
Fasten off, leaving a long tail for sewing. Stuff body.
With tail, sew body to bottom of head.

Lower Part of Shirt
Round 1 Hold Gnome upside down (legs in the air), join I with sc in any of the un-worked front loops at back of Round 8 of body, sc in remaining 23 sc—24 sc.
Rounds 2–7 Sc in each sc around.
Sl st in next sc.
Fasten off.

Arm (make 2)
Beginning at hand, with G, ch 2.
Round 1 (right side) 4 sc in 2nd ch from hook; do not join, work in continuous rounds—4 sc. Place a marker for beginning of round and move marker up as work progresses.
Round 2 Work 2 sc in each sc around—8 sc.
Rounds 3 and 4 Sc in each sc around; change to I in last st of Round 4.
Round 5 Sc in each sc around.
Round 6 BPsc in each sc around.
Stuff arm as Rounds 7–13 are worked.
Rounds 7–13 Sc in each sc around.
Fasten off, leaving a long tail for sewing. Flatten open end and sew closed. Sew arm to side of body, near where body meets head.

Legs (make 2)
Beginning at boot, with K, ch 2.
Round 1 (right side) 5 sc in 2nd ch from hook; do not join, work in continuous rounds—5 sc. Place a marker for beginning of round and move marker up as work progresses.
Round 2 Sc in each sc around—10 sc.

Fairy & Gnome Dolls

Round 3 Sc in next 3 sc, dc in next 4 sc, sc in next 3 sc.

Rounds 4 and 5 Sc in next 3 sc, hdc in next 4 sts, sc in next 3 sc.

Rounds 6 and 7 Sc in each st around; change to J in last st of Round 7. Stuff boot.

Round 8 BPsc in each sc around. Stuff leg as Rounds 9-14 are worked.

Rounds 9–14 Sc in each sc around. Fasten off, leaving a long tail for sewing. Sew leg to bottom of body.

Hat

Beginning at top of hat, with H, ch 2.

Round 1 (right side) 6 sc in 2nd ch from hook; do not join, work in continuous rounds—6 sc. Place a marker for beginning of round and move marker up as work progresses.

Round 2 Work 2 sc in each sc around—12 sc.

Round 3 Sc in each sc around.

Round 4 [Sc in next sc, 2 sc in next sc] 6 times—18 sc.

Round 5 Sc in each sc around.

Round 6 [Sc in next 2 sc, 2 sc in next sc] 6 times—24 sc.

Round 7 Sc in each sc around.

Round 8 [Sc in next 3 sc, 2 sc in next sc] 6 times—30 sc.

Round 9 Sc in each sc around.

Round 10 [Sc in next 4 sc, 2 sc in next sc] 6 times—36 sc.

Round 11–15 Sc in each sc around.

Round 16 [Sc in next 5 sc, 2 sc in next sc] 6 times—42 sc.

Rounds 17–21 Sc in each sc around. Sl st in next sc.
Fasten off.

Belt

With K, ch 35 loosely.

Row 1 Dc in 3rd ch from hook, dc in each remaining ch across—33 dc.
Fasten off.
Wrap belt around Gnome's waist. With brown embroidery floss, sew belt in place and embroider a buckle.

FINISHING

Beard

Work sts around the post of sts across lower part of face, as follows: Join F with sl st in side of head where you want the beard to begin. Working on the side of face, *ch 4, sl st around post of next st; repeat from * down side of face to front of face; working across front of face, **ch 8, sl st around post of next st; repeat from ** across front of face to other side of face; work up other side of face in same manner as for first side of beard. Repeat this process back and forth across lower part of face until beard is desired thickness. Weave in all ends. ■

MATERIALS

Yarn (4)

RED HEART® *Sport*, 2½oz/70g skeins, each approx 165yd/150m (acrylic)

1 skein each:
- #316 Soft White (A)
- #912 Cherry Red (B)
- #230 Yellow (C)
- #816 Wedgewood Blue (D)

Note Only small amounts of B, C, and D are needed.

Hooks
- Size F/5 (3.75mm) crochet hook
- Size E/4 (3.5mm) crochet hook (for pocket watch only)

Notions
- Stitch marker
- Small piece of red craft felt (for hearts)
- Small piece of white craft felt (for watch face)
- Two 9mm safety eyes
- Small amount of black embroidery floss (for nose and mouth)
- Small amount of blue embroidery floss (for pocket watch hands)
- Embroidery needle
- Polyester fiberfill
- Sewing needle, red sewing thread (for sewing felt hearts to tunic), and white sewing thread (for sewing face to pocket watch)
- Yarn needle

FINISHED MEASUREMENTS

Rabbit Approx 8"/20.5cm tall (from bottom to tips of ears)

GAUGE

Gauge is not critical for this project.

NOTES

1 Work tightly so stuffing will not show through stitches.

2 Rounds are worked in continuous spirals. Do not join at end of rounds, and do not turn at beginning of rounds.

3 To change color, work last stitch of old color to last yarn over. Yarn over with new color and draw through all loops on hook to complete stitch. Fasten off old color and proceed with new color.

MUZZLE

With larger hook and A, ch 2.

Round 1 (right side) 6 sc in 2nd ch from hook; do not join, work in continuous rounds—6 sc. Place a marker for beginning of round and move marker up as work progresses.

Round 2 Work 2 sc in each sc around—12 sc.

Round 3 [Sc in next sc, 2 sc in next sc] 6 times—18 sc.

Rounds 4–6 Sc in each sc around. Fasten off, leaving a long tail for sewing. With black embroidery floss, and using photograph as a guide, embroider nose and mouth on muzzle.

HEAD

Beginning at top of head, with larger hook and A, ch 2.

Round 1 (right side) 6 sc in 2nd ch from hook; do not join, work in continuous rounds—6 sc. Place a marker for beginning of round and move marker up as work progresses.

Round 2 Work 2 sc in each sc around—12 sc.

Round 3 [Sc in next sc, 2 sc in next sc] 6 times—18 sc.

Round 4 [Sc in next 2 sc, 2 sc in next sc] 6 times—24 sc.

Round 5 [Sc in next 3 sc, 2 sc in next sc] 6 times—30 sc.

Round 6 [Sc in next 4 sc, 2 sc in next sc] 6 times—36 sc.

Round 7 [Sc in next 5 sc, 2 sc in next sc] 6 times—42 sc.

Round 8 [Sc in next 6 sc, 2 sc in next sc] 6 times—48 sc.

Rounds 9–19 Sc in each sc around.

Round 20 [Sc in next 6 sc, sc2tog] 6 times—42 sc.

Round 21 [Sc in next 5 sc, sc2tog] 6 times—36 sc.

Round 22 [Sc in next 4 sc, sc2tog] 6 times—30 sc.

Stuff muzzle and sew to front of head. Attach safety eyes.

Round 23 [Sc in next 3 sc, sc2tog] 6 times—24 sc.
Round 24 Sc in each sc around.
Round 25 [Sc in next 2 sc, sc2tog] 6 times—18 sc.
Stuff head firmly.
Round 26 [Sc in next sc, sc2tog] 6 times—12 sc.
Round 27 [Sc2tog] 6 times—6 sc.
Fasten off and weave in end.

EAR (MAKE 2)
With larger hook and A, ch 2.
Round 1 (right side) 6 sc in 2nd ch from hook; do not join, work in continuous rounds—6 sc. Place a marker for beginning of round and move marker up as work progresses.
Round 2 Sc in each sc around.
Round 3 Work 2 sc in each sc around—12 sc.
Rounds 4–13 Sc in each sc around.
Sl st in next sc.
Fasten off, leaving a long tail for sewing. Sew ears to top of head.

BODY
Beginning at bottom of body, with larger hook and A, ch 2.
Rounds 1–6 Work Rounds 1–6 of head—36 sc.
Rounds 7–18 Sc in each sc around.
Fasten off, leaving a long tail for sewing. Stuff body. With tail, sew body to bottom of head.

Arms and Legs (make 2 each)
With larger hook and A, ch 5.
Rounds 1 and 2 Work Rounds 1 and 2 of head—12 sc.
Rounds 3–11 Sc in each sc around.
Fasten off, leaving a long tail for sewing. Flatten open end and use long tail to sew top closed. With tail, sew arms and legs to body.

Tail
With larger hook and A, ch 2.
Rounds 1–5 Work Rounds 1–5 of arm—12 sc.
Round 6 [Sc2tog] 6 times—6 sc.

Fasten off, leaving a long tail for sewing. With tail, sew to back of body.

TUNIC
Beginning at top of tunic, with larger hook and B, ch 33, loosely.
Row 1 (right side) Sc in 2nd ch from hook and in each remaining ch across—32 sc. Fasten off.
Note The front, shoulders, and back will be worked back and forth in rows over only some of the 32 sc of Row 1.

Back
Row 2 (wrong side) With wrong side of Row 1 facing and larger hook, join C with sc in first sc, sc in next 9 sc; leave remaining sts unworked for shoulders and front—10 sc.
Rows 3–8 Ch 1, turn, sc in each sc across; change to B in last st of Row 8. Fasten off.
Row 9 With B, ch 1, turn, sc in each sc across. Fasten off.

First Shoulder
Row 2 (wrong side) With wrong side facing and larger hook, join C with sc in first unworked sc of Row 1 following back, sc in next 5 sc; leave remaining sts unworked for front and second shoulder—6 sc.
Rows 3 and 4 Ch 1, turn, sc in each sc across; change to B in last st of Row 4. Fasten off.
Row 5 With B, ch 1, turn, sc in each sc across. Fasten off.

Front
Row 2 (wrong side) With wrong side facing and larger hook, join C with sc in first unworked sc of Row 1 following first shoulder, sc in next 9 sc; leave remaining sts unworked for second shoulder—10 sc.
Rows 3–9 Work Rows 3–9 of back. Fasten off.

Second Shoulder
Row 2 (wrong side) With wrong side facing and larger hook, join C with sc in first unworked sc of Row 1 following front, sc in next 5 sc—6 sc.

Rows 3–5 Work Rows 3–5 of first shoulder. Fasten off.

TIE (MAKE 2)
With larger hook, join B with sl st in top corner of back (not joined to a shoulder), ch 15.
Fasten off. Repeat on top corner of second shoulder.
Cut three small hearts from red felt. Sew 1 heart to back of tunic, and 2 small hearts to front.

Bow
With larger hook and D, ch 17, loosely.
Row 1 Hdc in 3rd ch from hook and in each remaining ch across—15 hdc. Fasten off. Sew ends together to form a ring. Flatten bow, placing seam at center back.

Bow Wrap
With larger hook and D, ch 6, loosely
Row 1 Sc in 2nd ch from hook and in each remaining ch across—5 sc. Fasten off. Wrap around center of bow and sew ends together. Sew bow to one shoulder of tunic.

Rabbit

POCKET WATCH

With smaller hook and C, ch 2.

Round 1 (right side) 5 sc in 2nd ch from hook; do not join, work in continuous rounds—5 sc. Place a marker for beginning of round and move marker up as work progresses.

Round 2 Work 2 sc in each sc around—10 sc.

Round 3 [Sc in next sc, 2 sc in next sc] 5 times—15 sc.

Round 4 [Sc in next 2 sc, 2 sc in next sc] 5 times—20 sc.

Round 5 [Sc in next 3 sc, 2 sc in next sc] 5 times—25 sc.

Rounds 6 and 7 Working in back loops only, sc in each sc around.

Cut a circle from white felt. With blue embroidery floss, using photograph as a guide, embroider pocket watch hands. Sew felt circle centered on right side of pocket watch.

Round 8 [Sc in next 3 sc, sc2tog] 5 times—20 sts.

Round 9 [Sc in next 2 sc, sc2tog] 5 times—15 sts.

Round 10 [Sc in next sc, sc2tog] 5 times—10 sts.

Stuff pocket watch lightly.

Round 11 [Sc2tog] 5 times—5 sts.

Fasten off, leaving a long tail. Thread tail through stitches of last round and pull to close opening. Weave in end.

Pocket Watch Chain

With C, ch 7. Fasten off and sew one end of chain to pocket watch and the other end to the rabbit's hand.

FINISHING

Weave in all ends. Place tunic around rabbit's neck and knot ties into a bow. ■

Big Apple

MATERIALS

Yarn [4]

RED HEART® Super Saver®, 7oz/198g skeins, each approx 364yd/333m (acrylic)

1 skein each:
- #319 Cherry Red (A)
- #321 Gold (B)
- #400 Grey Heather (C)
- #312 Black (D)
- #336 Warm Brown (E)

Hooks
- Size G/6 (4mm) crochet hook *or any size to obtain correct gauge*
- Size E/4 (3.5mm) crochet hook

Notions
- Black and white craft felt
- White sequins for Bridge "lights"
- Polyester fiberfill
- White and black sewing thread
- Sewing needle
- Black embroidery floss
- 3 pairs of black 12mm plastic eyes with safety backings
- Stitch marker
- Yarn needle

FINISHED MEASUREMENTS

Heart Approx 6½"/16.5cm high x 6.5"/16.5cm wide

Taxi Approx 6½"/16.5cm long x 2½"/6.5cm wide x 5"/12.5cm high

Bridge Approx 10½"/26.5cm long x 4½"/11.5cm wide x 7"/18cm high

GAUGE

16 sc and 19 sc rows = 4"/10cm.
Take time to check gauge.

NOTE

Larger hook is used throughout, except for Bridge Railings and Bridge Hanging Wires.

HEART

Starting at bottom with A, ch 2.

Round 1 (right side) Work 6 sc in 2nd ch from hook—6 sc. Do not join. Work in a continuous spiral. Place stitch marker in first st and move up to first st in each round as work progresses.

Round 2 Work 2 sc in each sc around—12 sc.

Round 3 [Sc in next sc, 2 sc in next sc] 6 times—18 sc.

Round 4 Sc in each sc around.

Round 5 [Sc in next 2 sc, 2 sc in next sc] 6 times—24 sc.

Round 6 Sc in each sc around.

Round 7 [Sc in next 3 sc, 2 sc in next sc] 6 times—30 sc.

Round 8 Sc in each sc around.

Round 9 [Sc in next 4 sc, 2 sc in next sc] 6 times—36 sc.

Round 10 Sc in each sc around.

Round 11 [Sc in next 5 sc, 2 sc in next sc] 6 times—42 sc.

Round 12 Sc in each sc around.

Round 13 [Sc in next 6 sc, 2 sc in next sc] 6 times—48 sc.

Big Apple

Round 14 Sc in each sc around.
Round 15 [Sc in next 7 sc, 2 sc in next sc] 6 times—54 sc.
Round 16 Sc in each sc around.
Round 17 [Sc in next 8 sc, 2 sc in next sc] 6 times—60 sc.
Rounds 18–27 Sc in each sc around.

First Top Curve

Round 28 Sk next 30 sc, sc in next 30 sc—30 sc.
Round 29 Sc in each sc around.
Round 30 [Sc in next 3 sc, sc2tog] 6 times—24 sc.
Round 31 Sc in each sc around.
Round 32 [Sc in next 2 sc, sc2tog] 6 times—18 sc.
Round 33 Sc in each sc around.
Round 34 [Sc in next sc, sc2tog] 6 times—12 sc.
Round 35 Sc in each sc around.
Round 36 [Sc2tog] 6 times, sl st in next sc—6 sc. Fasten off, leaving a long tail. Weave tail through stitches to close up hole. Position and attach plastic eyes with safety backings between Rounds 17 and 18. With embroidery floss, embroider mouth, as shown in photograph. Stuff as much of Heart as you can, especially top of First Top Curve.

Second Top Curve

Round 28 With right side facing, join A with sl st in first unworked sc on Round 27, ch 1, sc in same sc as joining and in next 29 unworked sc—30 sc.
Rounds 29–36 Repeat Rounds 29–36 on First Top Curve, stuffing as you go.

FINISHING

Sew space between top curves closed. Weave in ends.

TAXI

Sides (make 2)

Starting at top with B, ch 9 loosely.
Row 1 (wrong side) Sc in 2nd ch from hook and in each remaining ch across—8 sc.
Row 2 (right side) Ch 1, turn; 2 sc in first sc, sc in each sc across to last sc, 2 sc in last sc—10 sc.
Rows 3–5 Repeat Row 2, 3 more

times—16 sc at end of Row 5 (2 more sc in each row).
Rows 6–11 Ch 1, turn; sc in each sc across.
Rows 12–18 Repeat Row 2, 7 more times—30 sc at end of Row 18.
Row 19 Ch 1, turn; sc in each sc across.

Wheel Wells, Front End

Row 20 Ch 1, turn; sc in first 4 sc, leaving last 26 sc unworked—4 sc.
Rows 21 and 22 Ch 1, turn; sc in each sc across. At end of Row 22, fasten off.

Wheel Wells, Back End

Row 20 With wrong side facing, join B with sl st in first sc on Row 19, ch 1, sc in same st as joining and in next 3 sc, leaving last 22 sc unworked—4 sc.
Rows 21 and 22 Ch 1, turn; sc in each sc across. At end of Row 22, fasten off.

Center

Row 20 With wrong right facing, sk next 4 unworked sc on Row 19 after Front End of Wheel Wells, join B with sl st in next sc, ch 1, sc in same sc as joining, sc in next 13 sc, leaving last 4 sc unworked—14 sc.
Rows 21 and 22 Ch 1, turn; sc in each sc across. At end of Row 22, fasten off. Referring to photo throughout, cut 2 windows for each side out of white felt and sew in place with black sewing thread. With embroidery floss, embroider door outline. With C, embroider door handle.
Note Work Side door and window details as mirror images, so both Sides face to the front when Taxi is assembled.

Wheels (make 4)

With C, ch 2.
Round 1 (right side) Work 5 sc in 2nd ch from hook, changing to D in last sc—5 sc. Do not join. Place stitch marker in first st and move up to first st in each round as work progresses.
Round 2 With D, work 2 sc in each sc around—10 sc.
Round 3 [Sc in next sc, 2 sc in next sc] 5 times—15 sc.
Rounds 4 and 5 Sc in back loop of each sc around.
Round 6 [Sc in next sc, sc2tog] 5 times—10 sc. Stuff Wheel.
Round 7 [Sc2tog] 5 times—5 sc. Fasten off, leaving a long tail. Weave tail through stitches to close up hole.

Roof

With B, ch 11 loosely.
Row 1 Sc in 2nd ch from hook and in each remaining ch across—10 sc.
Rows 2–32 Ch 1, turn; sc in each sc across. At end of Row 32, fasten off, leaving a long tail for sewing. Center and sew side edges of Roof to top edges of Sides.

Front and Back (make 2)

With B, ch 11 loosely.
Rows 1–11 Work same as Rows 1–11 on Roof. At end of Row 11, fasten off, leaving a long tail for sewing.
Cut front windshield and back window out of white felt. With black sewing thread, sew in place on Front and Back. Cut 2 circles from white felt slightly larger than plastic eyes. Position and attach plastic eyes with safety backings to Front, with white felt behind eyes, as shown in photo. With embroider floss, sew mouth on Front. Sew side edges of Front and Back to remaining side edges of Sides and remaining edges of Roof. With Round 1 of Wheels facing outside of Taxi, sew Wheels in place in space of Wheel Wells on Sides, using remaining front loops on Round 5 of Wheels.

Fenders (make 4)

With B, ch 12 loosely.
Row 1 (right side) Hdc in 3rd ch from hook (skipped chs do not count as a st),

hdc in each remaining ch across—10 hdc. Fasten off, leaving a long tail for sewing. Sew side edge of Fender to top of Wheels, as shown in photo.

Bottom
With D, ch 11 loosely.
Row 1 Sc in 2nd ch from hook and in each remaining ch across—10 sc.
Row 2 Ch 1, turn; 2 sc in first sc, sc in each sc across to last sc, 2 sc in last sc—12 sc.
Row 3 Repeat Row 2—14 sc.
Rows 4–29 Ch 1, turn; sc in each sc across.
Row 30 Ch 1, turn; sc2tog, sc in each sc across to last 2 sc, sc2tog—12 sc.
Row 31 Repeat Row 30—10 sc. Fasten off, leaving a long tail for sewing. Sew edges of Bottom to bottom edges of Taxi Cab, stuffing as you go.

Taxi Sign
With embroidery floss, embroider "TAXI" on a small piece of white felt. With white sewing thread, sew white felt to a slighter larger piece of black felt. With black sewing thread, sew bottom edge of Taxi Sign to top center of Roof.

FINISHING
Weave in all ends.

BROOKLYN BRIDGE
First End, Front and Back (make 2)
Starting at top with E, ch 19 loosely.
Row 1 (wrong side) Sc in 2nd ch from hook and in each remaining ch across—18 sc.
Row 2 (right side) Ch 1, turn; sc in each sc across.
Rows 3–7 Repeat Row 2, 5 more times.

Right Pillar
Row 8 Ch 1, turn; sc in first 5 sc, leaving last 13 sc unworked—5 sc.
Row 9 Ch 1, turn; sc2tog, sc in last 3 sc—4 sc.
Row 10 Ch 1, turn; sc in first 2 sc, sc2tog—3 sc.
Rows 11–37 Ch 1, turn; sc in each sc across. At end of last row, fasten off.

Left Pillar
Row 8 With wrong side facing, join E with sl st in first sc in Row 7, ch 1, sc in same sc as joining and in next 4 sc, leaving remaining 8 sc unworked—5 sc.
Rows 9–37 Work same as Rows 9–37 on Right Pillar.

Middle Pillar
Row 8 With wrong side facing, sk next sc after Left Pillar, join E with sl st in next sc, ch 1, sc in same sc as joining and in next 5 sc, leaving last sc unworked—6 sc.
Row 9 Ch 1, turn; sc2tog, sc in next 2 sc, sc2tog—4 sc.
Row 10 Ch 1, turn; [sc2tog] twice—2 sc.
Rows 11–37 Ch 1, turn; sc in each sc. At end of last row, fasten off.
Position and attach plastic eyes with safety backings around Row 3. With embroidery floss, embroider mouth, as shown in photograph.

Outer Sides (make 2)
With E, ch 5 loosely.
Row 1 Sc in 2nd ch from hook and in each remaining ch across—4 sc.
Rows 2–37 Ch 1, turn; sc in each sc across. At end of last row, fasten off, leaving a long tail for sewing. Sew Outer Sides to sides of Front and Back of Bridge from top of Bridge to bottom of Left and Right Pillars.

Inside Pillar Sides (make 4)
With E, ch 5 loosely.
Row 1 Sc in 2nd ch from hook and in each remaining ch across—4 sc.
Rows 2–30 Ch 1, turn; sc in each sc across. At end of last row, fasten off, leaving a long tail for sewing. Sew Inside Pillar Sides to inside edges of Right and Left Pillars, as well as both side edges of Middle Pillar on Front and Back pieces. Sew top edge of Inside Pillar Sides together at top of Pillars.

Bottom of Right and Left Pillars (make 2)
With E, ch 5 loosely.
Row 1 Sc in 2nd ch from hook and in each remaining ch across—4 sc.
Rows 2–4 Ch 1, turn; sc in each sc across. At end of last row, fasten off, leaving a long tail for sewing. Sew to bottom of Right and Left Pillars.

Big Apple

Bottom of Middle Pillar
With E, ch 5 loosely.
Rows 1–3 Work same as Rows 1–3 on Right and Left Pillars. At end of Row 3, fasten off, leaving a long tail for sewing. Sew to bottom of Middle Pillar.

Top
With E, ch 5 loosely.
Row 1 Sc in 2nd ch from hook and in each remaining ch across—4 sc.
Rows 2–21 Ch 1, turn; sc in each sc across. At end of last row, fasten off, leaving a long tail for sewing. Stuff Bridge End. Sew Top to top edges of assembled Bridge End.

Second Bridge End
Work same as First Bridge End, omitting eyes and mouth.

Road (make 2)
With C, ch 13 loosely.
Row 1 Sc in 2nd ch from hook and in each remaining ch across—12 sc.
Rows 2–39 Ch 1, turn; sc in each sc across. At end of last row, fasten off, leaving a long tail on one piece for sewing.

Place Road pieces together, one on top of the other. Sew pieces together around edges, stuffing as you go. Sew ends of Road between Bridge Ends, approx 1½"/4cm from bottom of Pillars on Bridge Ends, with eyes and mouth facing Road, as shown in photo.

Railings (make 2)
With E hook and C, ch 53 loosely.
Row 1 Dc in 3rd ch from hook (skipped chs do not count as a st); *ch 1, sk next ch, dc in next ch; repeat from * across—26 dc and 25 ch-1 sps. Fasten off, leaving a long tail for sewing. Sew bottom edge of Railings to side edges of Road.

Hanging Wires (make 4)
With E hook and D, ch 70 loosely. Fasten off. Sew ends of Hanging Wires to top, inside edge of Bridge Ends. With white sewing thread, sew 10 sequins evenly spaced across each of 2 outer Hanging Wires to simulate lights on Bridge, as shown in photo.

FINISHING
Weave in all ends. ■

Smiley Cones

FINISHED MEASUREMENTS

Approx 10"/25.5cm tall x 11"/28cm around (at widest point)

GAUGE

17 sc and 19 rounds = 4"/10cm using size G/6 (4mm) crochet hook. *Take time to check gauge.*

NOTES

1 This project is worked in continuous rounds. Do not join and do not turn after completing a round.

2 Use a stitch marker to mark the beginning of each round; move it up as each round is completed.

3 Be sure to work tightly to ensure a sturdy toy and to prevent fiberfill from showing through stitches.

4 When making toys for children under 3 years of age, do not use safety eyes or buttons. Instead, embroider features. Make sure all pieces are sewn together securely and yarn ends are completely woven in and trimmed when finished.

ICE CREAM SCOOP

With A, ch 3; join with sl st in first ch to form a ring.

Round 1 Work 7 sc into ring—7 sc.

Round 2 2 sc in each sc around—14 sc.

Round 3 [Sc in next sc, 2 sc in next sc] 7 times—21 sc.

Round 4 [Sc in next 2 sc, 2 sc in next sc] 7 times—28 sc.

Round 5 [Sc in next 3 sc, 2 sc in next sc] 7 times—35 sc.

Round 6 [Sc in next 4 sc, 2 sc in next sc] 7 times—42 sc.

Round 7 [Sc in next 5 sc, 2 sc in next sc] 7 times—49 sc.

Rounds 8–16 Sc in each sc around. Pause here to attach safety eyes and embroider mouth, using the photograph as a guide. Embroider the mouth using back stitches.

Round 17 [Sc2tog, sc in next 5 sc] 7 times—42 sc.

Round 18 [Sc2tog, sc in next 4 sc] 7 times—35 sc.

Round 19 [Sc2tog, sc in next 3 sc] 7 times—28 sc.

Round 20 (ruffle) Ch 3 (counts as first dc), 2 dc in same st, 3dc in each st around; join with sl st in top of beginning ch-3. Fasten off, leaving a long tail for sewing.

CHERRY

Note Leave at least a 3"/7.5cm tail when starting the cherry (for the stem).

Smiley Cones

With C, ch 3; join with sl st in first ch to form a ring.
Round 1 Work 7 sc into the ring —7 sc.
Round 2 2 sc in each sc around—14 sc.
Round 3 [Sc in next sc, 2 sc in next sc] 7 times—21 sc.
Rounds 4-6 Sc in each sc around.
Round 7 [Sc2tog, sc in next sc] 7 times—14 sc.
Fasten off, leaving a long tail for sewing.

Complete Stem
Use crochet hook to draw beginning yarn tail through original ring (if it is inside the cherry). Trim the yarn tail to approx 1¾"/4.5cm. Seal yarn end with a dab of clear nail polish or fabric glue.

CONE
With B, ch 3; join with sl st in first ch to form a ring.
Round 1 Work 7 sc into the ring—7 sc.
Round 2 2 sc in next sc, sc in next 6 sc—8 sc.
Note No longer use a stitch marker to mark the beginning of rounds. The remainder of the cone is worked in one long, continuous spiral.
Spiral rounds Sc in next 5 sc, 2 sc in next sc (increase made), sc in next 11 sc, 2 sc in next sc (increase made), sc in next 12 sc, 2 sc in next sc (increase made), sc in next 13 sc, 2 sc in next sc (increase made), sc in next 14 sc, continue working as established, working one more sc between increases, ending by working sc in next 33 sc, sl st in next sc.
Fasten off and weave in end.

FINISHING
Firmly stuff cherry. Place the open end of the cherry against the top of the ice cream. Using yarn needle and long yarn tail of cherry, sew cherry to top of ice cream. Firmly stuff ice cream and cone. Thread long yarn tail of ice cream up to Round 20 (base of dc ruffle) on interior of ice cream. Using yarn needle and long yarn tail of ice cream, whipstitch ice cream to cone. Weave in all ends. ■